Easy Baroque Guitar pieces

Compiled and edited by
Dmitrijs Volkovs

Access to Online Audio
https://esmistudio.com/guitarbook3.zip

Copyright © 2024 Dmitrijs Volkovs

ISBN: 978-1-7637136-5-9

Baroque Composers

Henry Purcell (1659-1695)

Henry Purcell was an English organist and Baroque composer of secular and sacred music. Although Purcell incorporated Italian and French stylistic elements into his compositions, his legacy was a uniquely English form of Baroque music.

Gaspar Sanz (1640-1710)

Gaspar Sanz was an Aragonese composer, guitarist, organist and priest born to a wealthy family in Calanda in the Spanish comarca of Bajo Aragón. He studied music, theology and philosophy at the University of Salamanca, where he was later appointed Professor of Music.

Johann Krieger (1651-1735)

Krieger's keyboard music places him among the most important German composers of his time. The two published collections, Sechs musicalische Partien (1697) and Anmuthige Clavier-Übung (1698), contain harpsichord suites, organ toccatas, fugues, ricercars, and other works. Krieger's contemporaries praised his contrapuntal skill, evident in the extant fugues and ricercars. Johann Mattheson was particularly impressed with Krieger's double fugues, remarking that he knew nobody who surpassed Krieger in this form, except Handel. Handel himself admired and studied Krieger's work, even taking a copy of Anmuthige Clavier-Übung with him to England.

CONTENTS

1 Baroque Era Composers

5 Aria *(Henry Purcell)*
6 Rujero *(Gaspar Sanz)*
7 Paradetas *(Gaspar Sanz)*
8 Bourree *(Johann Krieger)*
9 Menuet *(Johann Krieger)*
11 Menuet *(Johann Christoph Friederich Bach)*
12 Bourree *(Leopold Mozart)*
13 Españoleta *(Gaspar Sanz)*
16 Gigue *(Johann Anton Logy)*
17 Entree *(Giuseppe Antonio Brescianello)*
19 Gigue *(Giuseppe Antonio Brescianello)*
23 Preludium *(Robert de Visee)*
25 Bourrée - *Suite in D minor (Robert de Visée)*
26 Menuet *(Robert de Visée)*
27 Sarabande *(Robert de Visee)*
29 Allemande *(Robert de Visee)*
31 Gigue *(Robert de Visee)*
33 Menuet *(Silvius Leopold Weiss)*
34 Menuet I *(Silvius Leopold Weiss)*
35 Menuet II *(Silvius Leopold Weiss)*
36 Bourree *(Silvius Leopold Weiss)*
39 Sarabande *(Silvius Leopold Weiss)*
41 Menuet in G *(Johann Sebastian Bach)*
43 Bouree *(Johann Sebastian Bach)*
45 Gavotte *(Johann Sebastian Bach)*
49 Sarabande *(Johann Sebastian Bach)*
50 Preludium *(Johann Sebastian Bach)*

Johann Anton Logy (1645 – 1721)

Johann Anton Logy composed mostly dance suites. Losy mastered French **lute** style and his extant works demonstrate his intelligence, bright spirited love for the lute. His extensive and highly creative works are scattered through various archives

Johann Georg Leopold Mozart (1719 –1787)

Johann Georg Leopold Mozart was a German composer, conductor, teacher, and violinist. Mozart is best known today as the father and teacher of Wolfgang Amadeus Mozart, and for his violin textbook Versuch.

Robert de Visee (1655 – 1732)

Robert de Visée was a lutenist, guitarist, theorbist and viol player at the court of Louis XIV, as well as a singer, and composer for lute, theorbo and guitar. Robert de Visée's origin is unknown, although a Portuguese origin of his surname had been suggested. Visée published two books of guitar music which contained twelve suites between them, as well as a few isolated pieces.

Silvius Leopold Weiss (1687-1750)

Silvius Leopold Weiss was a German composer and lutenist. Weiss was one of the most important and most prolific composers of lute music in history and one of the best-known and most technically accomplished lutenists of his day. He wrote around 600 pieces for lute, most of them grouped into 'sonatas' or suites, which consist mostly of baroque dance pieces.

Johann Sebastian Bach (1685-1750)

Johann Sebastian Bach was a German composer, organist, harpsichordist, violist, and violinist whose sacred and secular works for choir, orchestra, and solo instruments drew together the strands of the Baroque period and brought it to its ultimate maturity.

Giuseppe Antonio Brescianello (1690-1758)

Giuseppe Antonio Brescianello was an Italian Baroque composer and violinist. He invigorated musical life in Stuttgart. His contemporaries praised his chamber works. The music of Brescianello shows great sense of melody, profound harmonic imagination combined with strong rhythmic element so typical to Italian school of the time.

Aria

Henry Purcell (1659 - 1695)

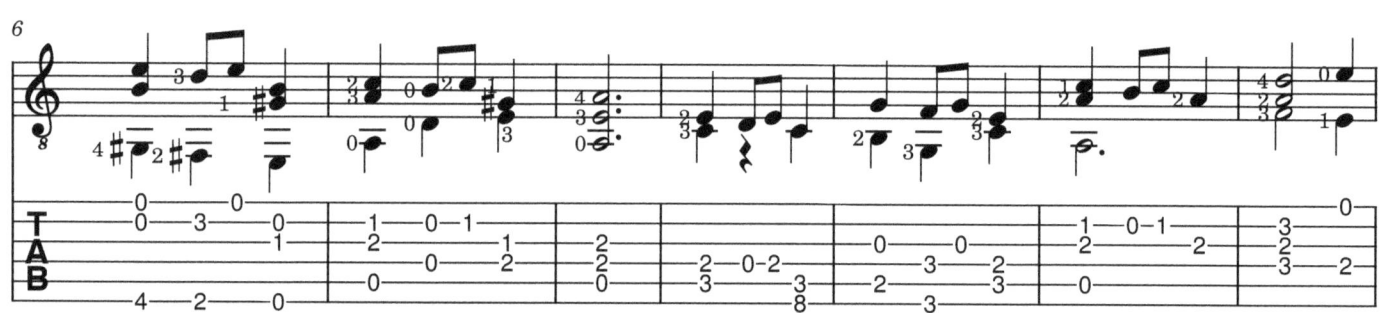

Rujero

Gaspar Sanz (1640-1710)

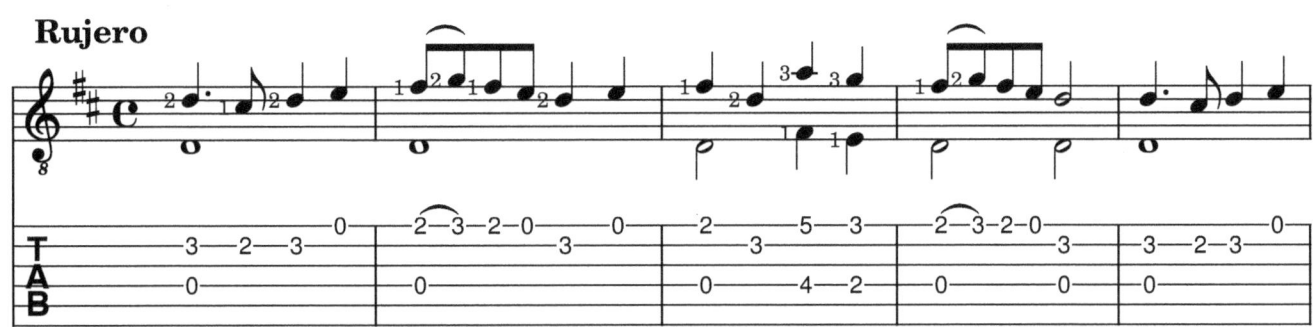
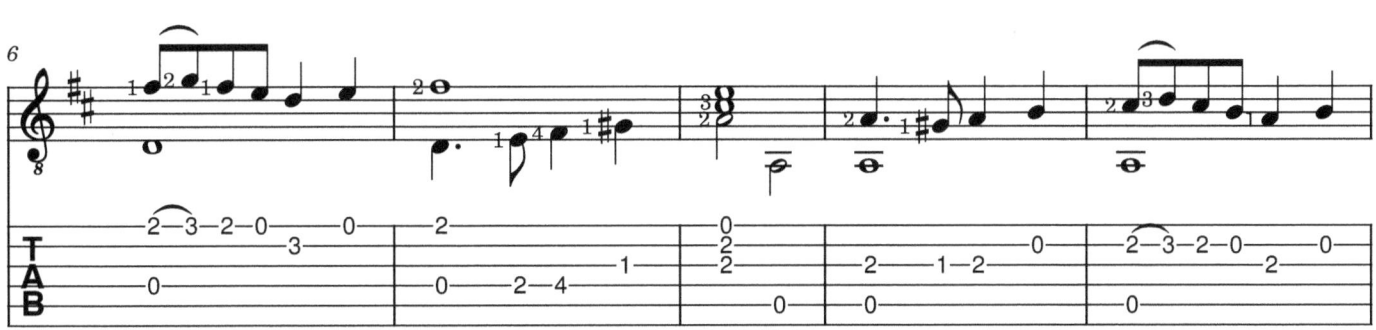
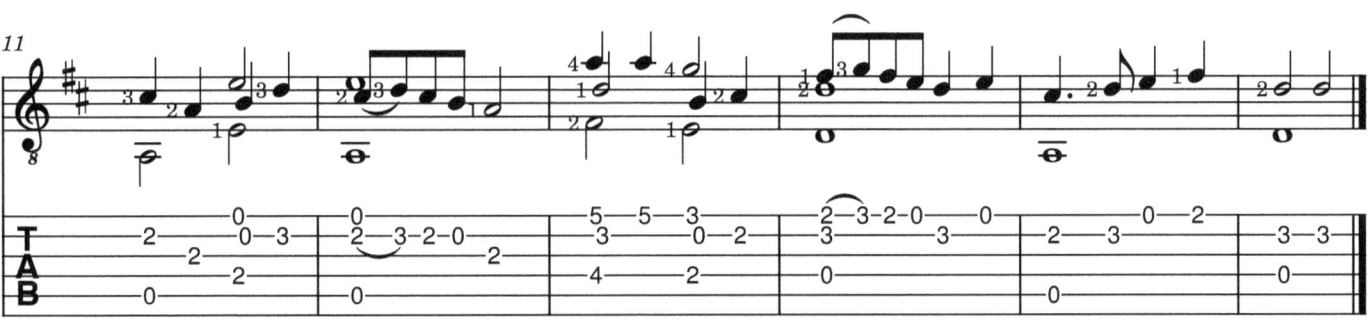

Paradetas

Gaspar Sanz (1640-1710)

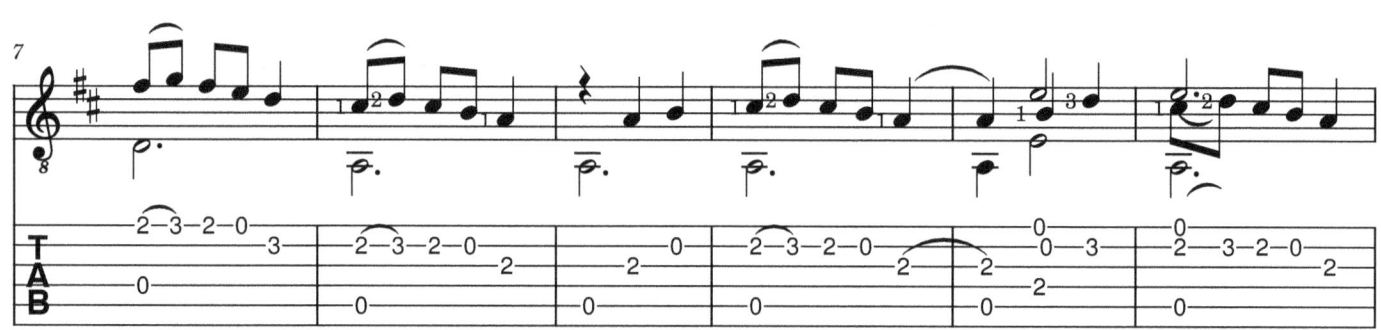

Bourrée

Johann Krieger (1651–1735)

Menuet

Johann Krieger (1651–1735)

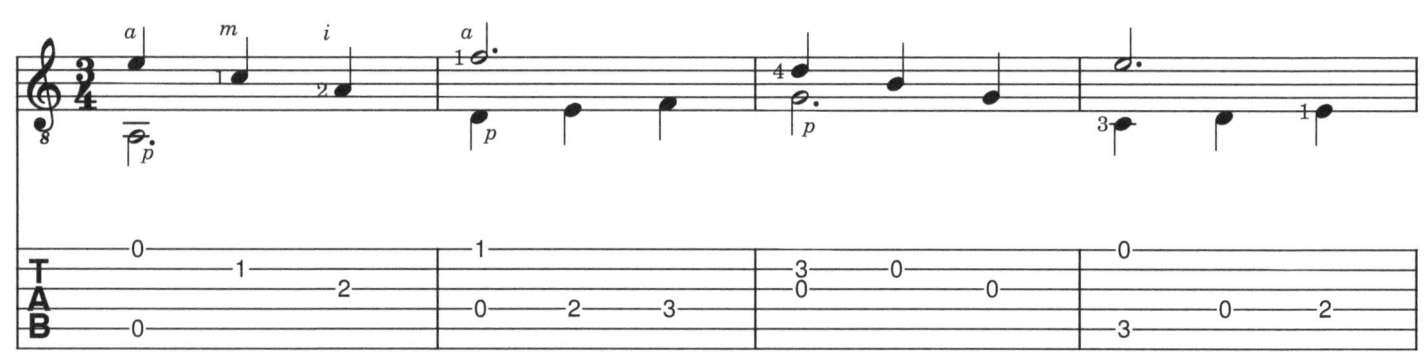

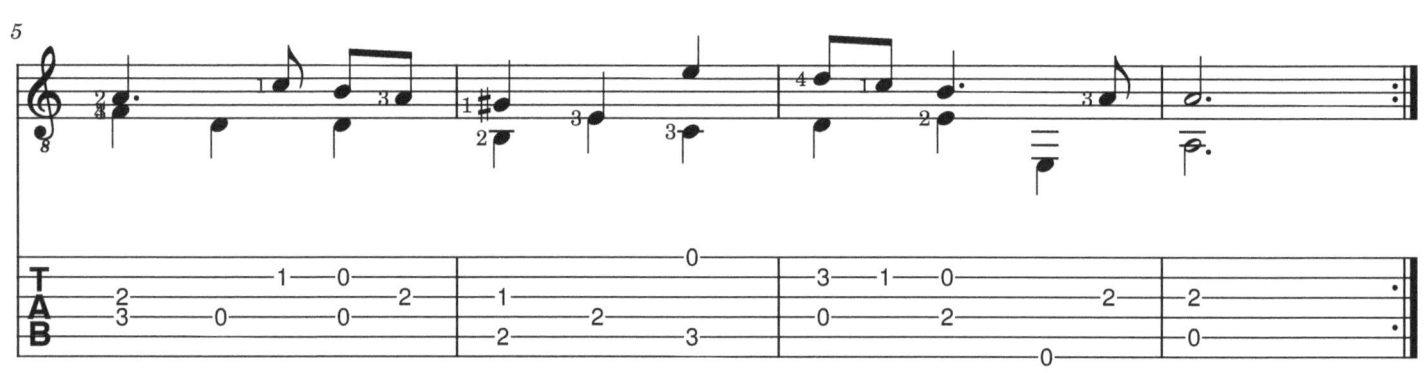

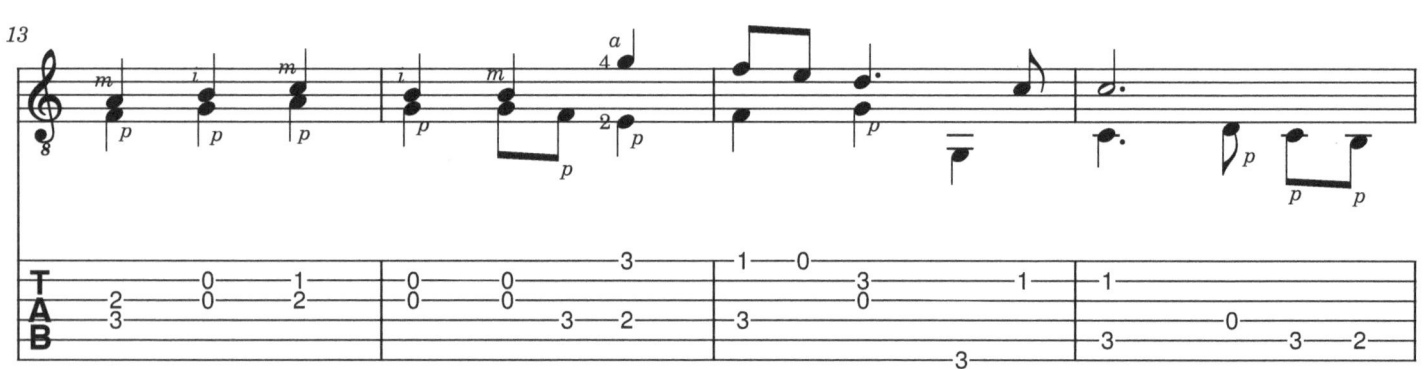

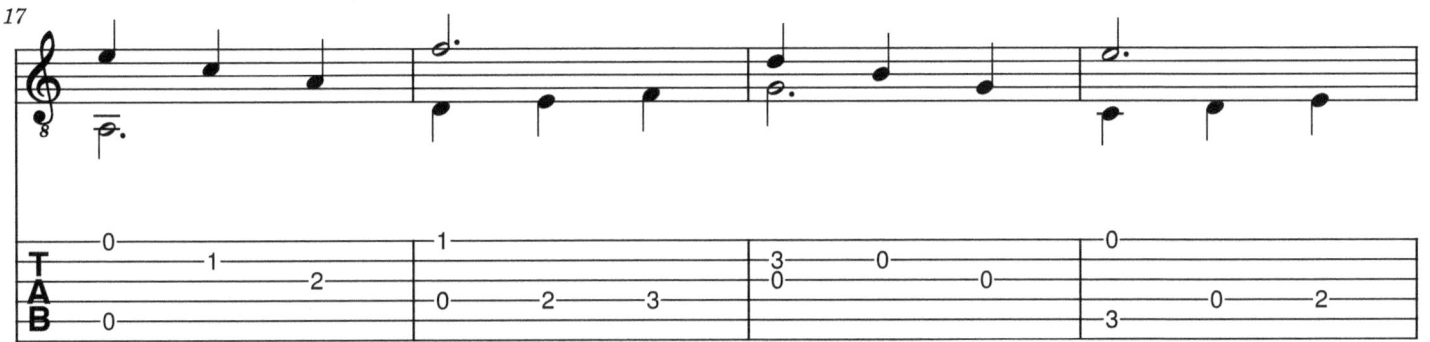

Menuet

Johann Christoph Friederich Bach (1732-1795)

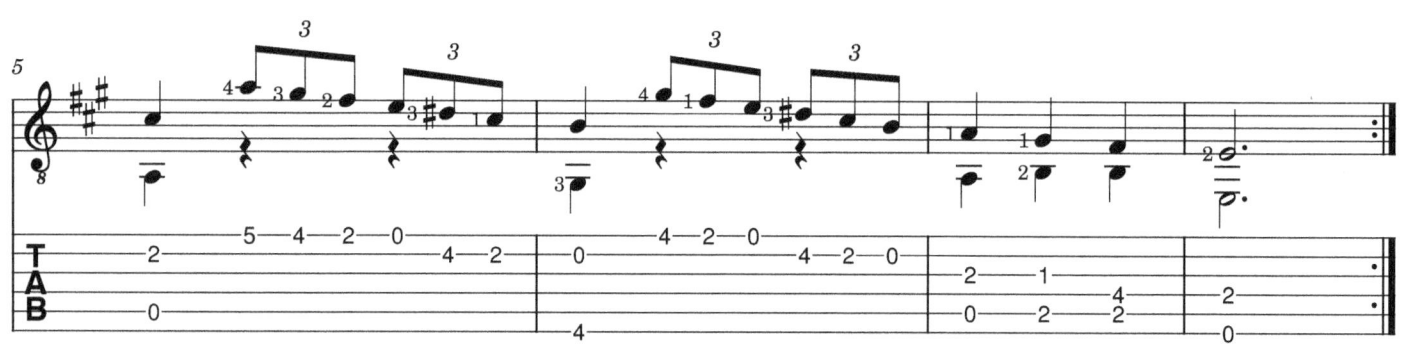

Bourree

Leopold Mozart (1719-1787)

Españoleta

Gaspar Sanz (1640-1710)

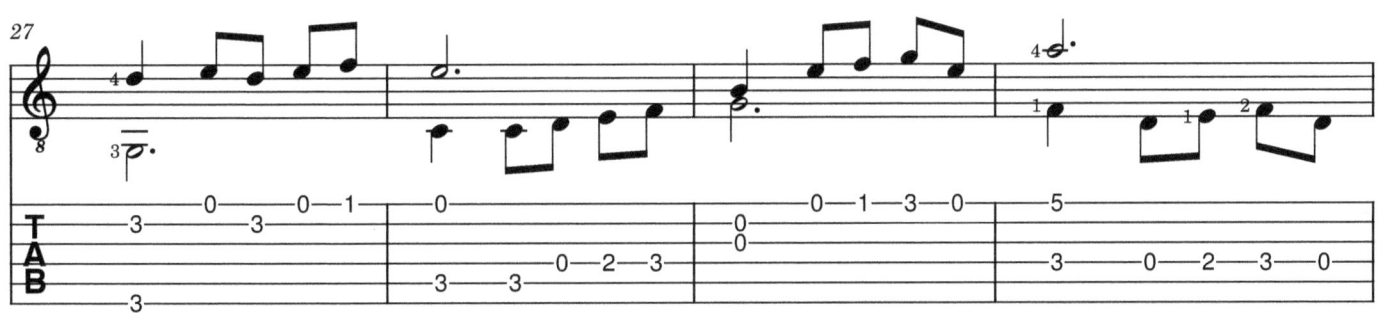
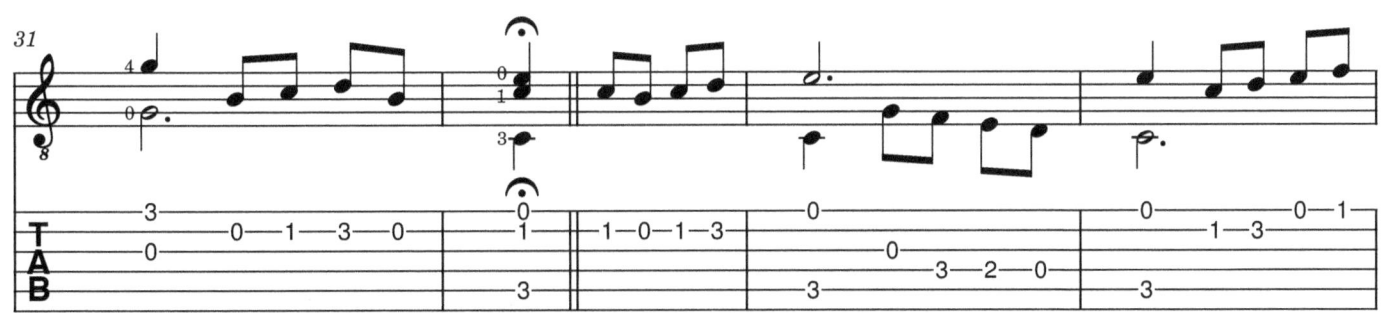

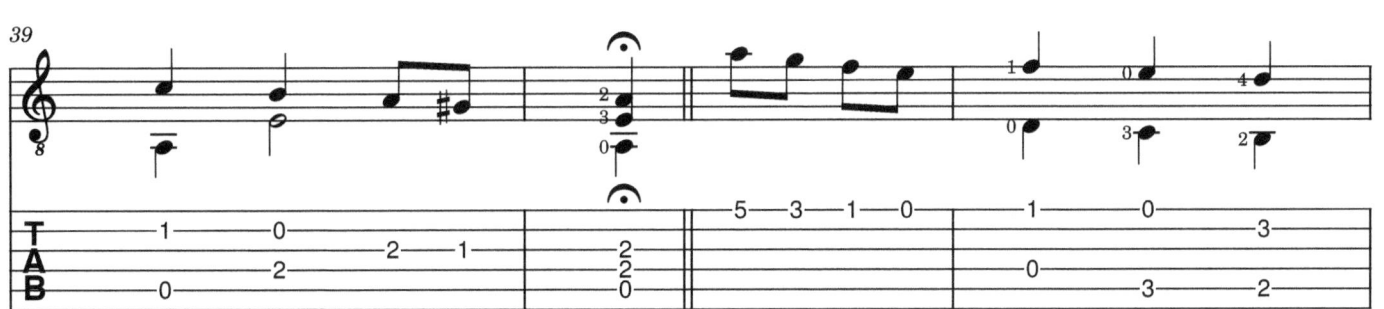

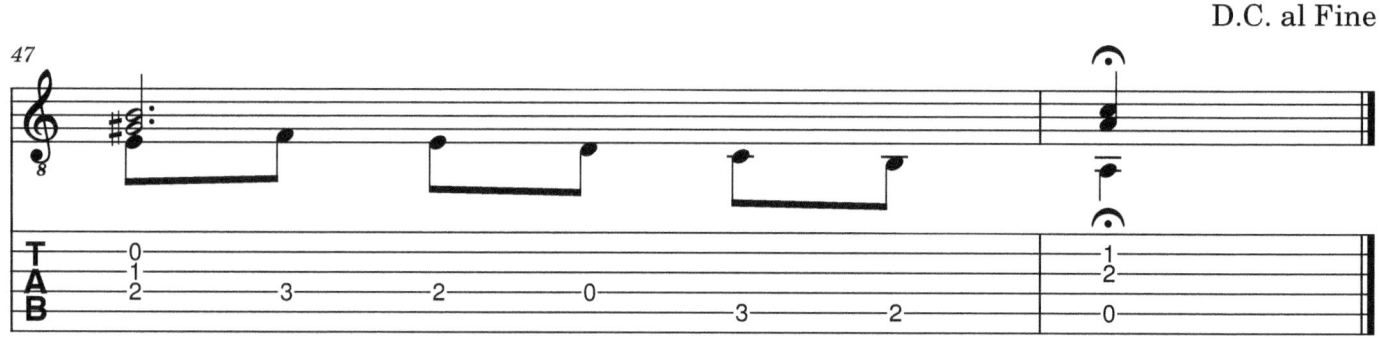

D.C. al Fine

Gigue

Johann Anton Logy (1650 - 1721)

Entrée

Giuseppe Antonio Brescianello (1690-1758)

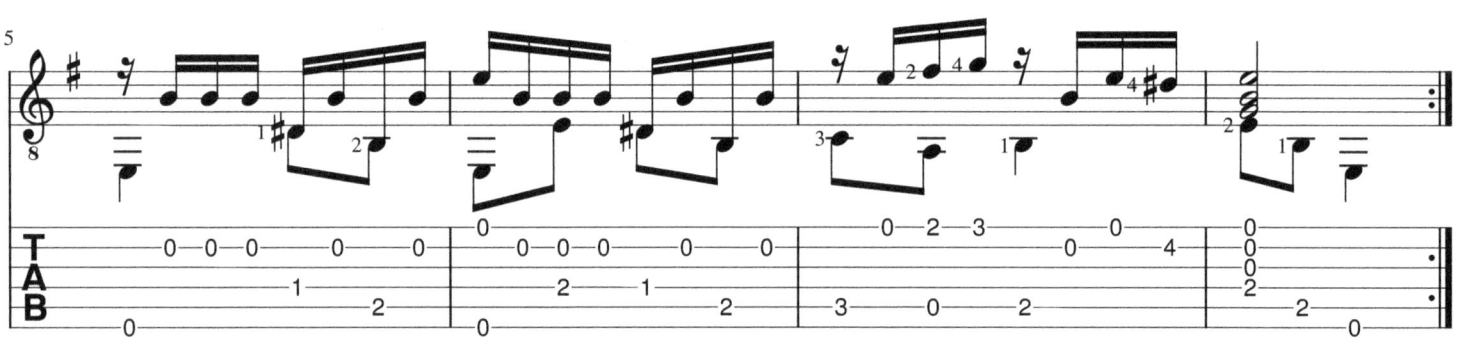
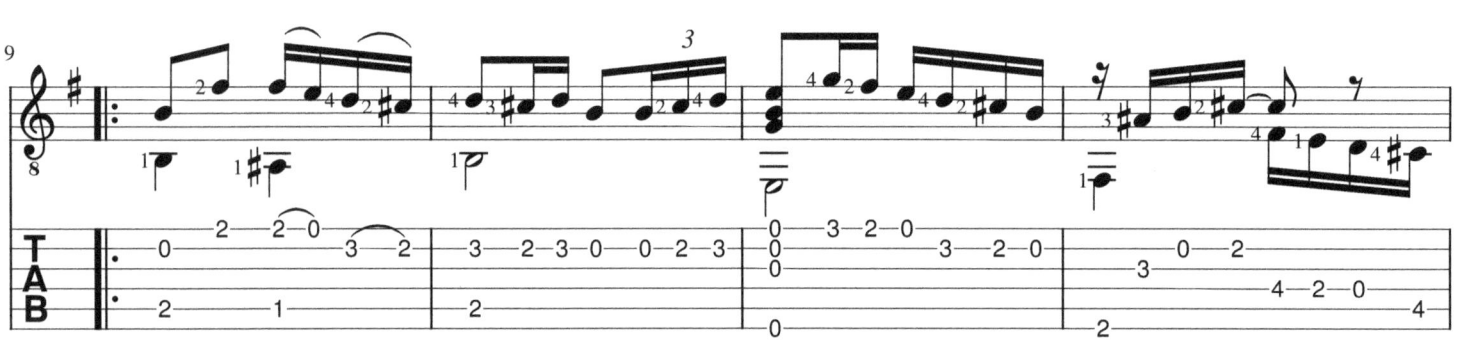

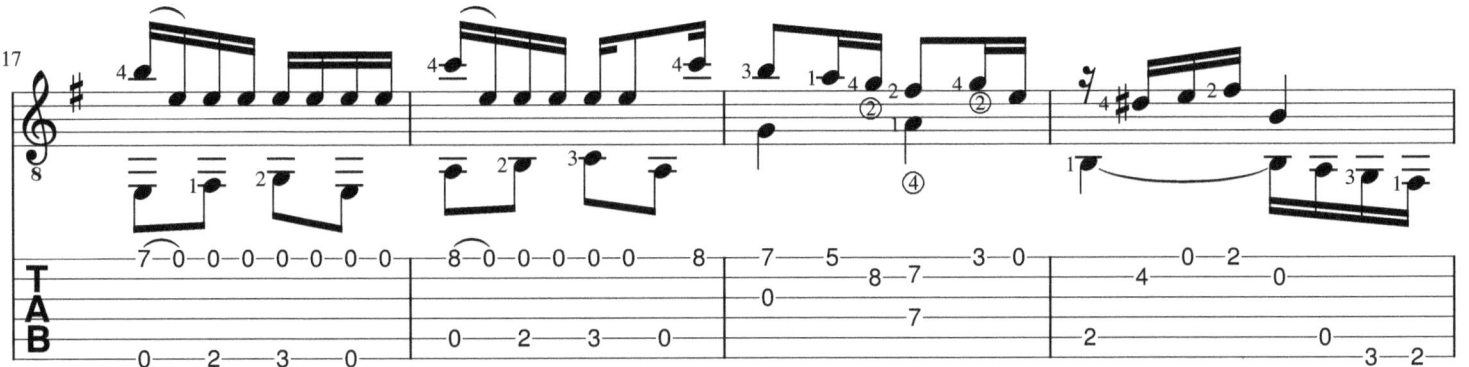
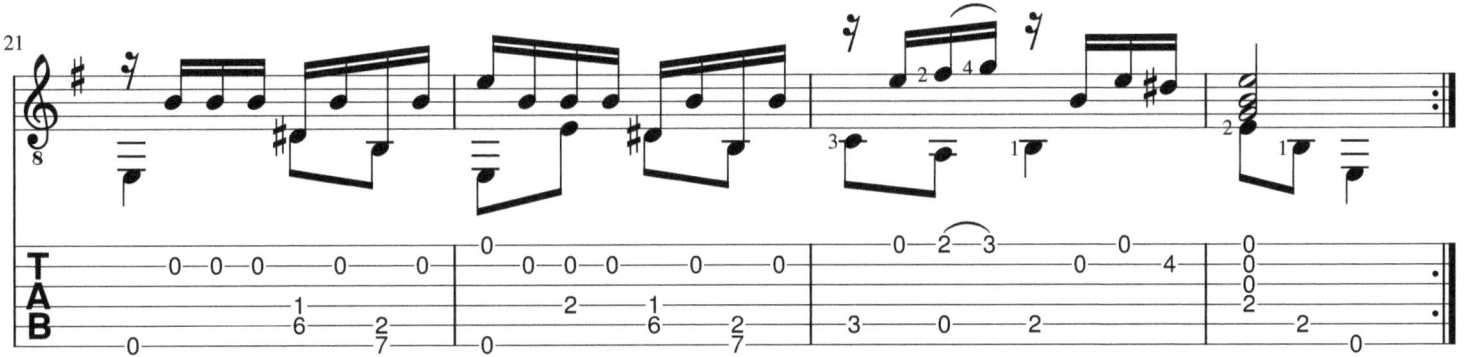

Gigue

Giuseppe Antonio Brescianello (1690-1758)

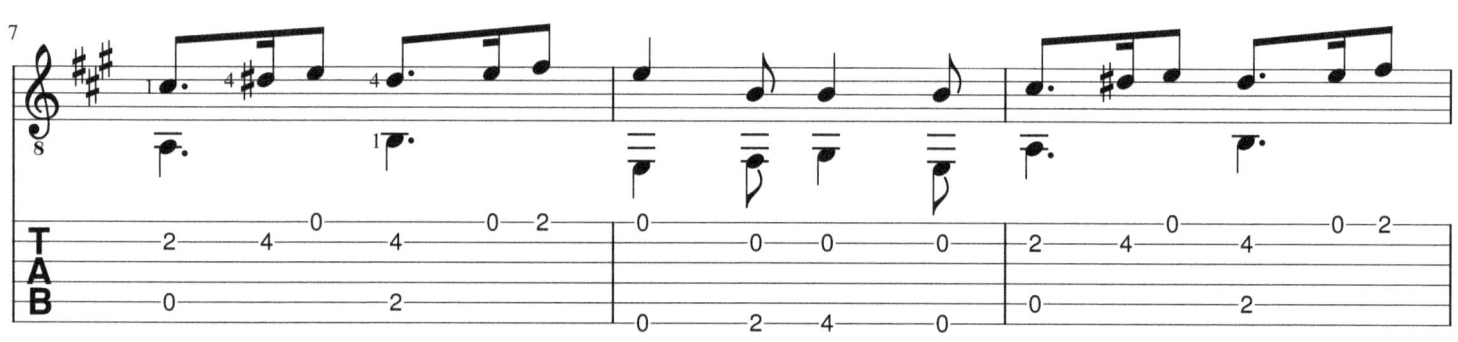

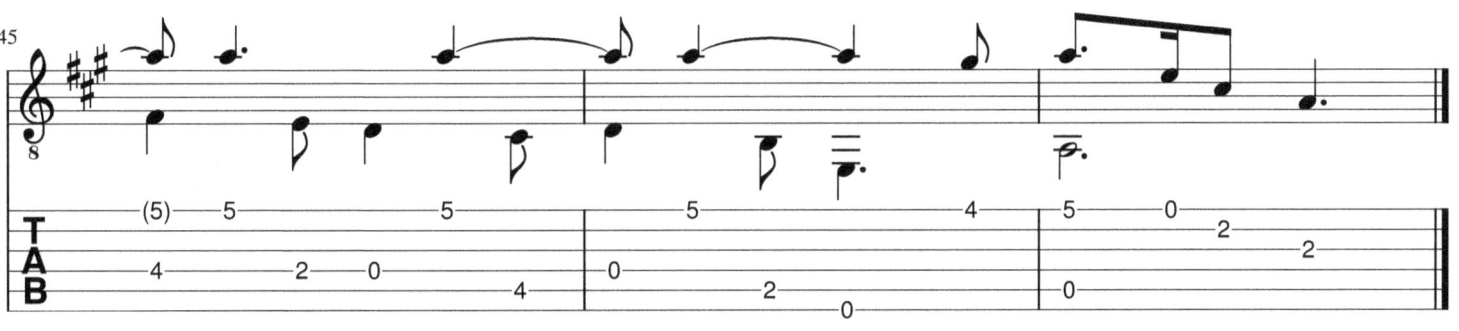

Preludium

Robert de Visée (1650-1725)

Bourrée - Suite in D minor

Robert de Visée (1650-1725)

Menuet

Robert de Visée (1650-1725)

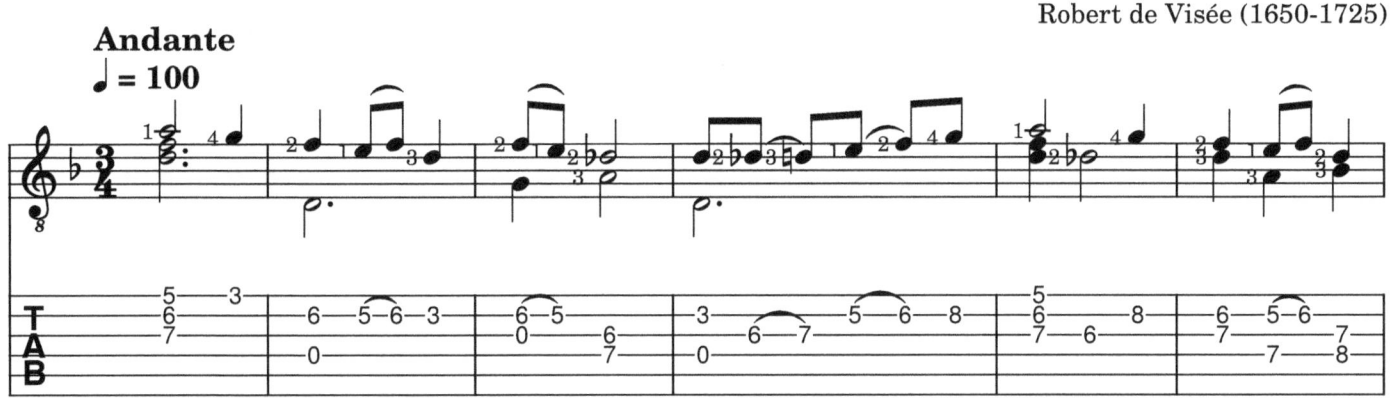
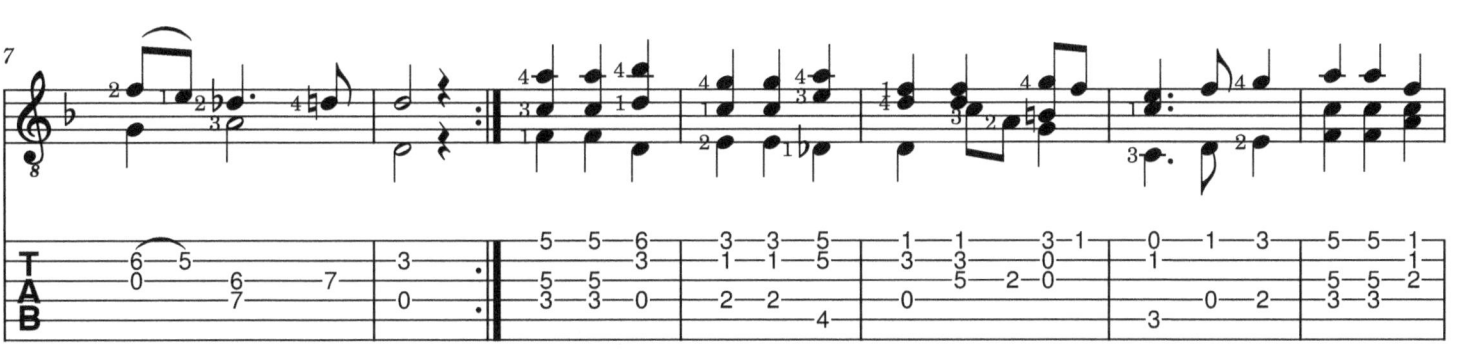

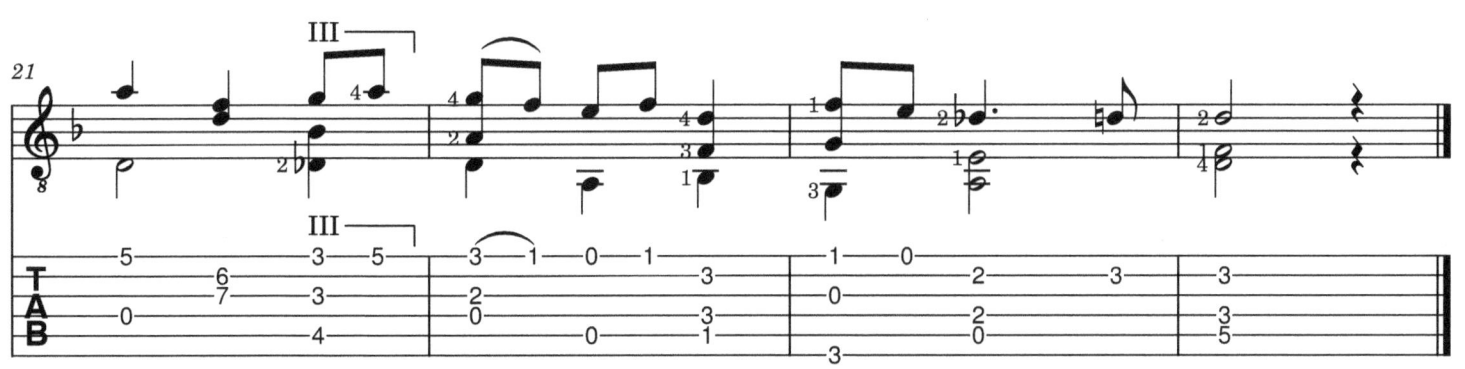

Sarabande

Robert de Visée (1650-1725)

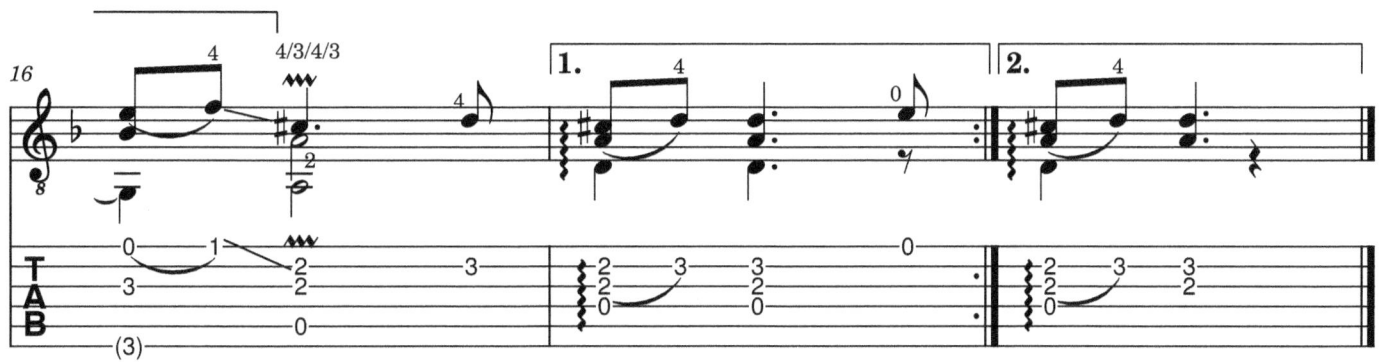

Allemande

Robert de Visée (1650-1725)

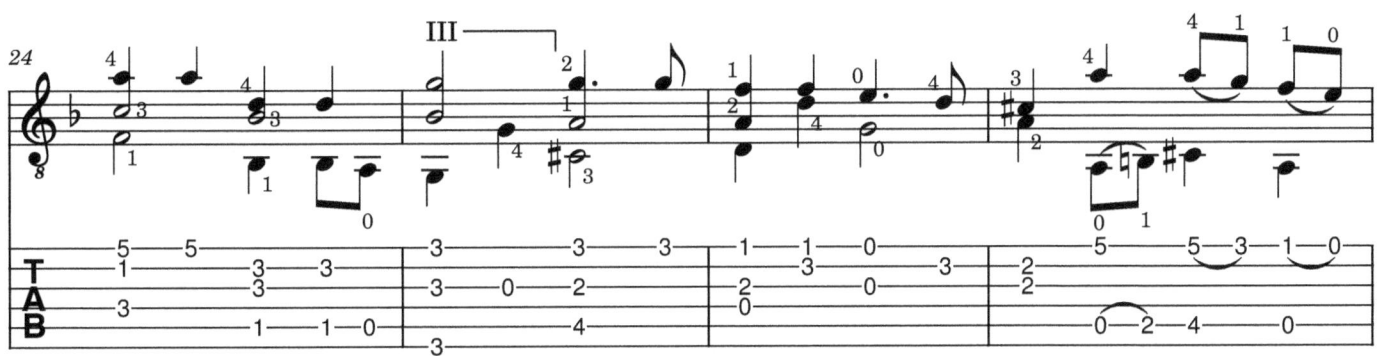
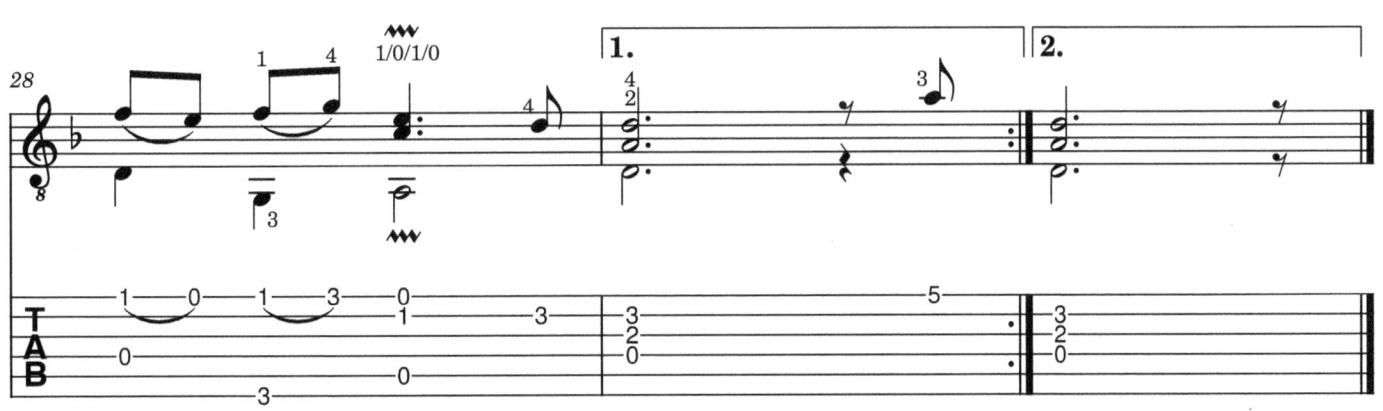

Gigue

Robert de Visée (1650-1725)

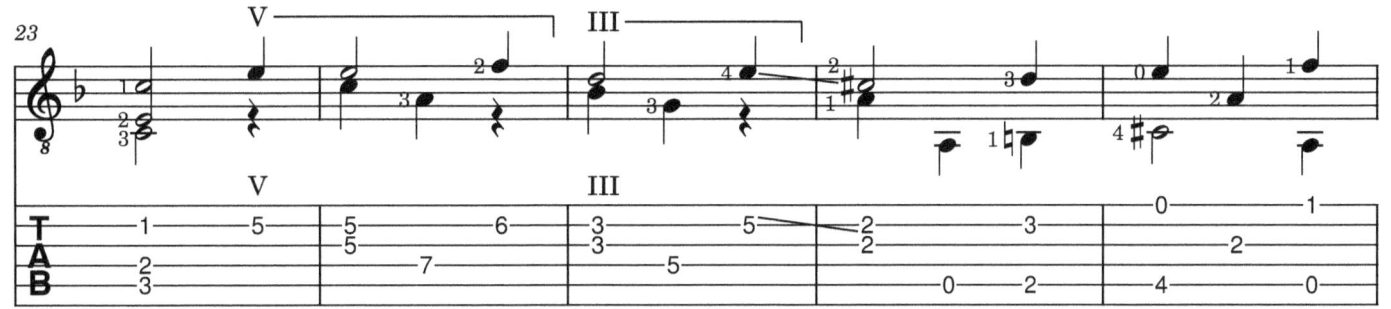

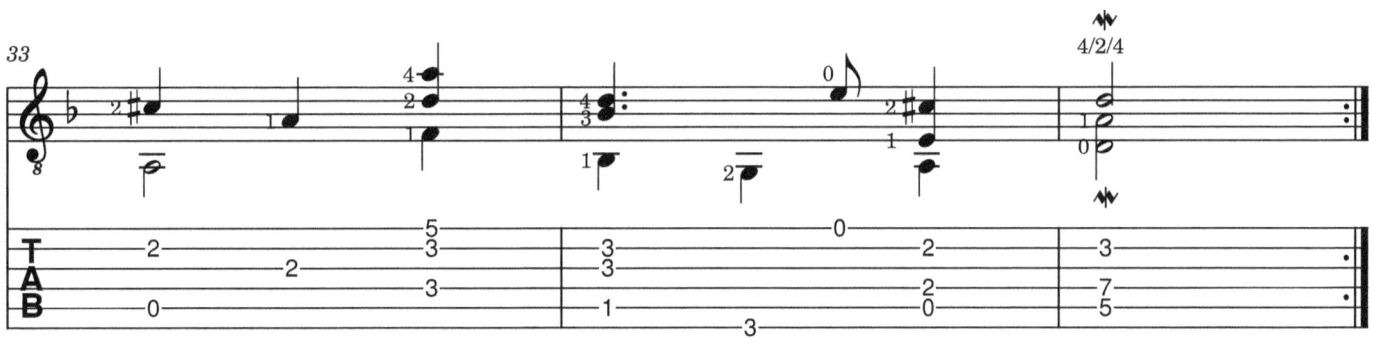

Menuet

Silvius Leopold Weiss (1687-1750)

Menuet

Silvius Leopold Weiss (1687-1750)

Menuet II

Silvius Leopold Weiss (1687-1750)

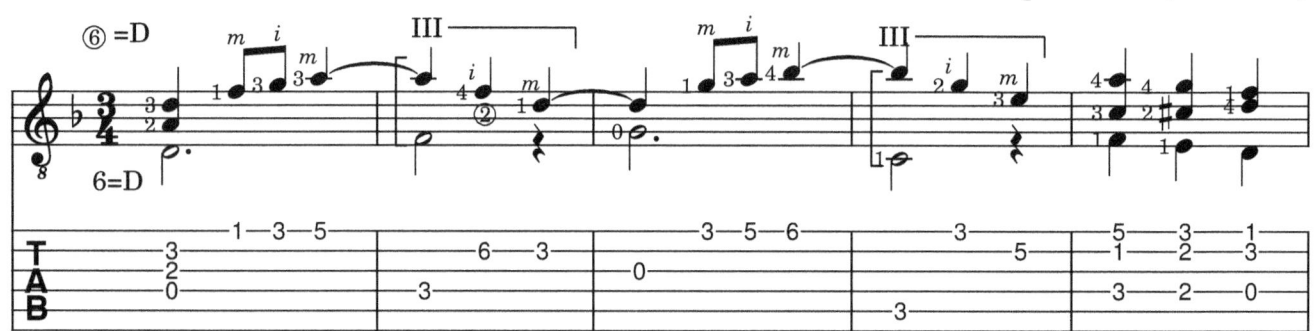

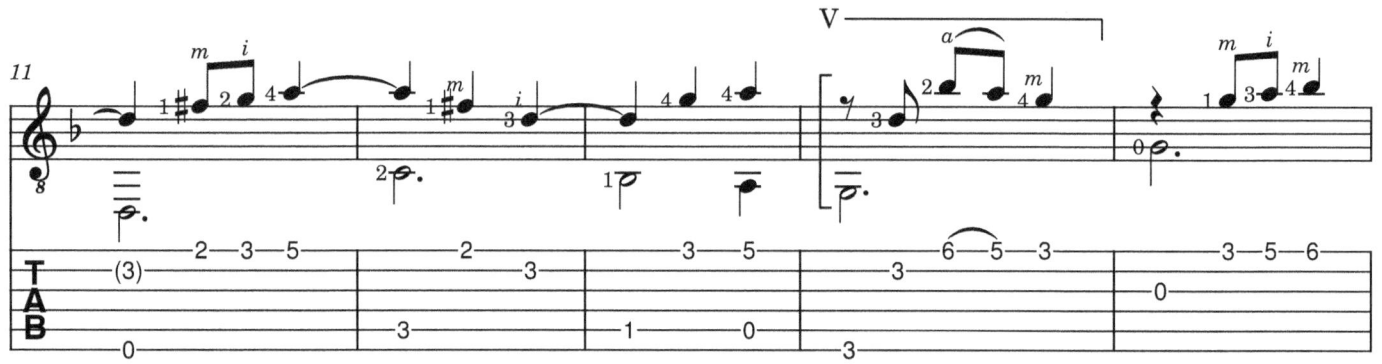
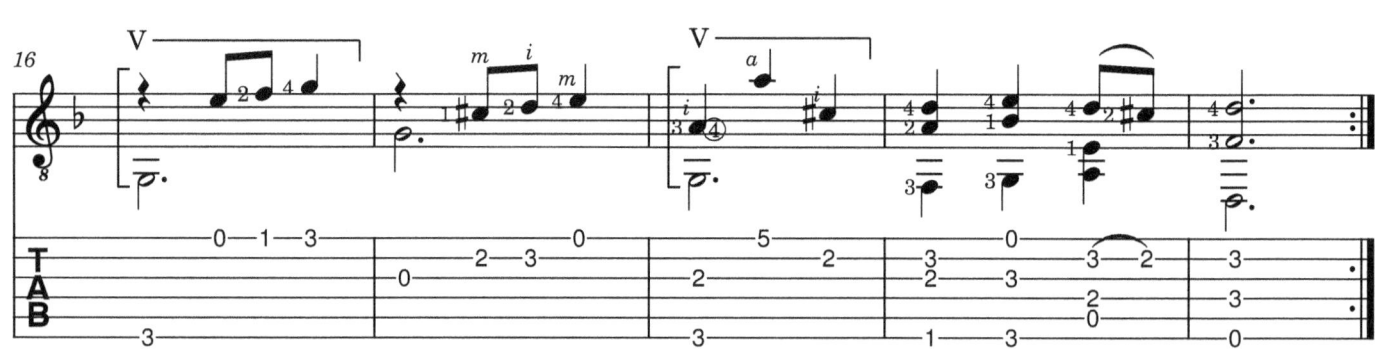

Bourree

Silvius Leopold Weiss (1687-1750)

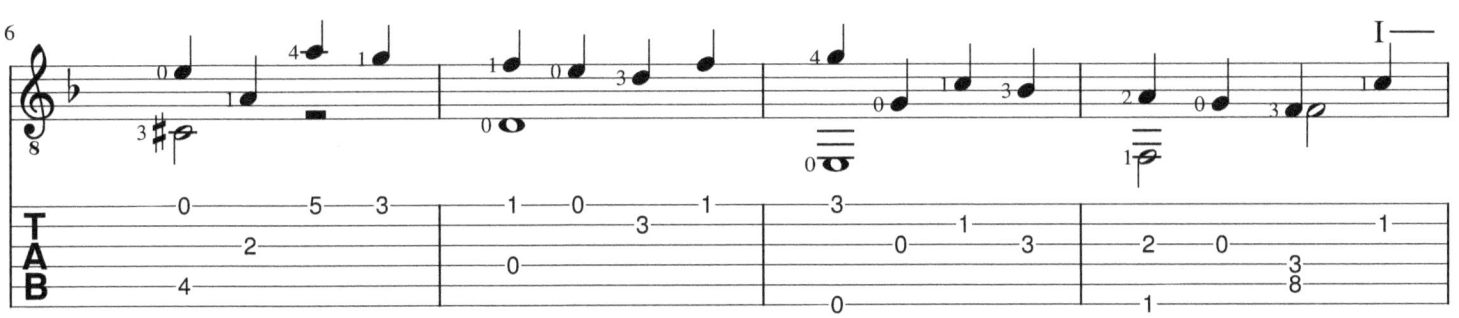
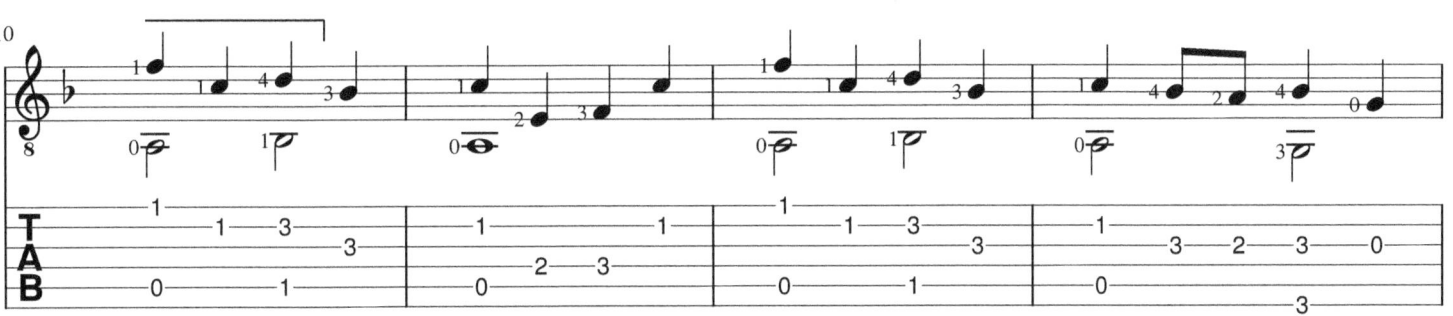
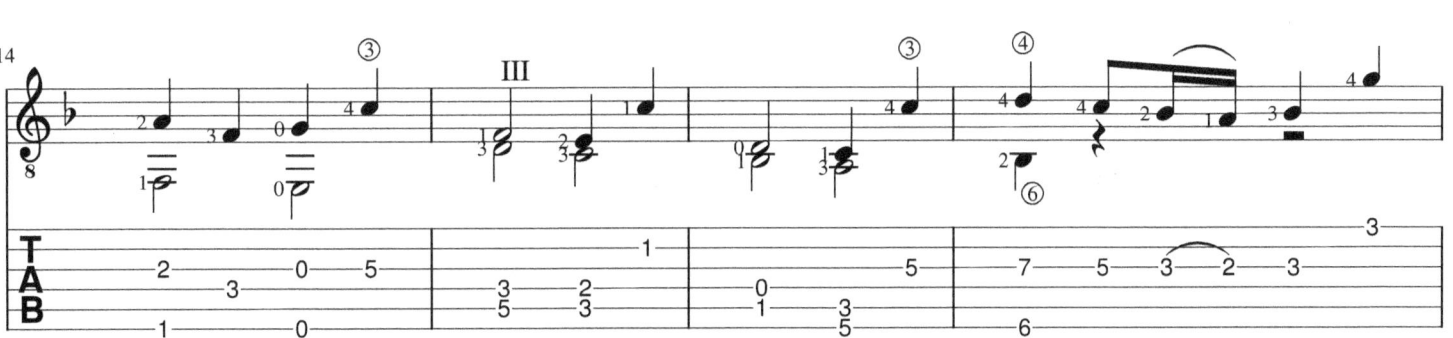

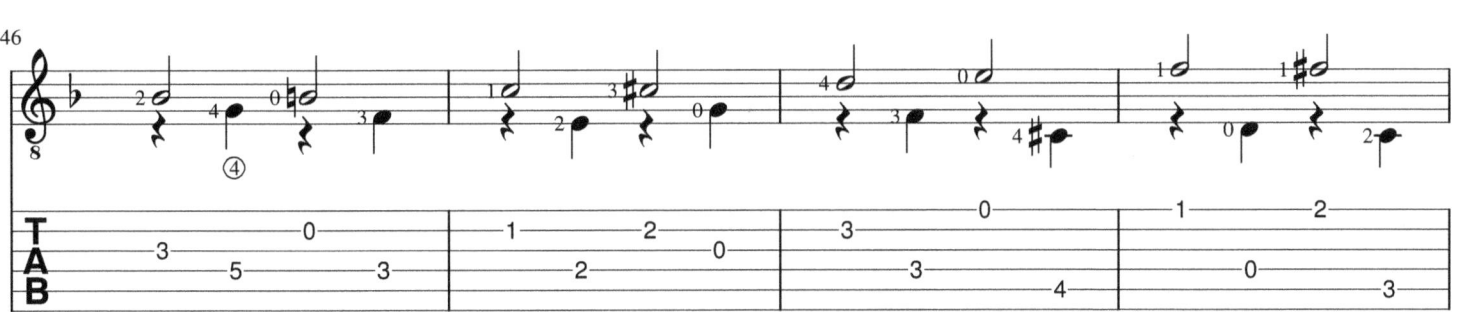
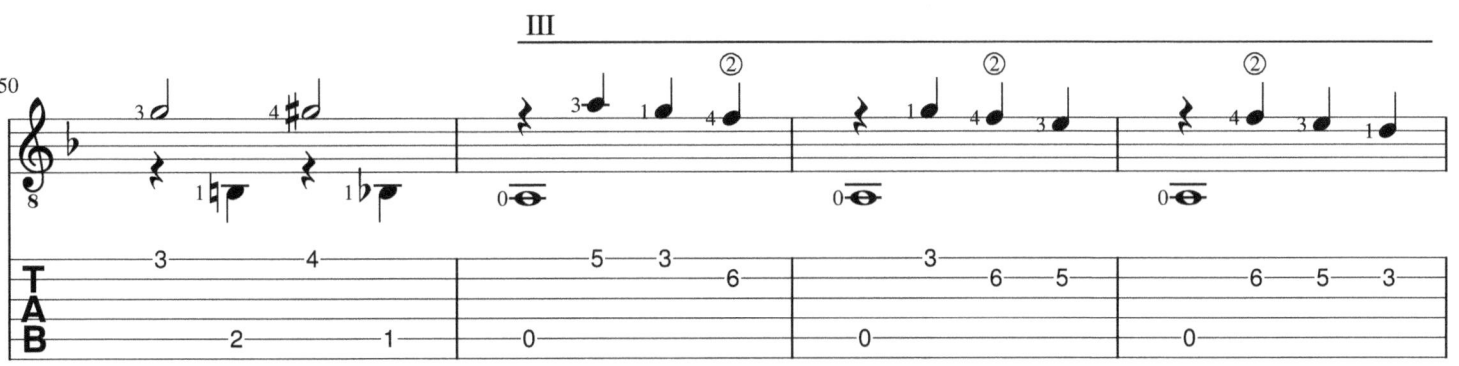
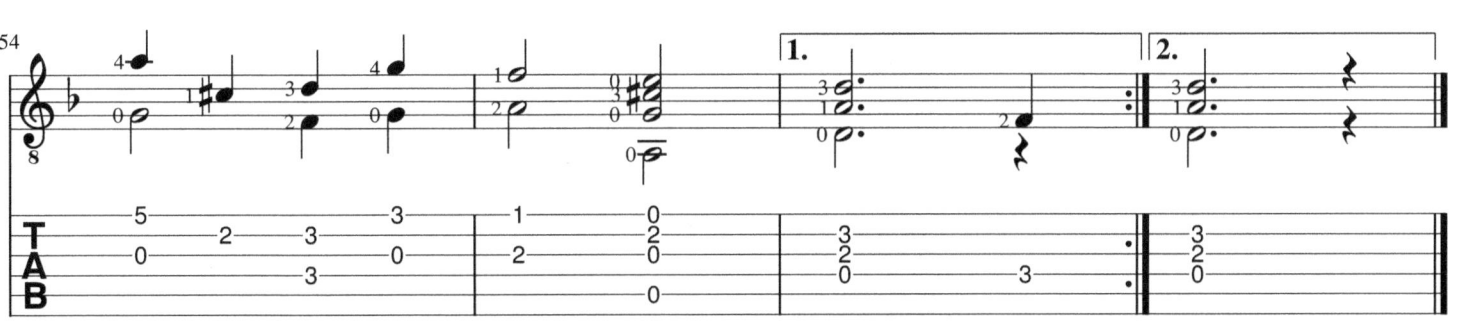

Sarabande

Silvius Leopold Weiss (1687-1750)

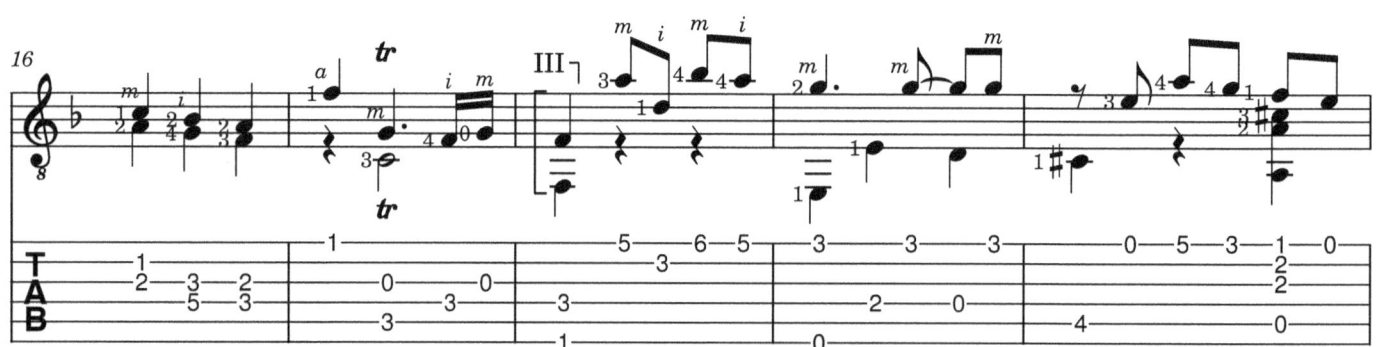

Menuet in G

Johann Sebastian Bach (1685-1750) BWV Anh. 114

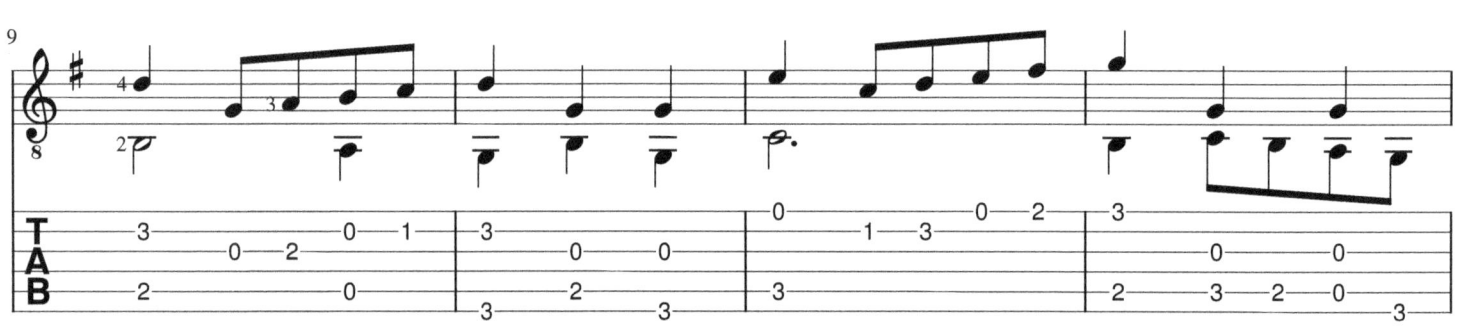
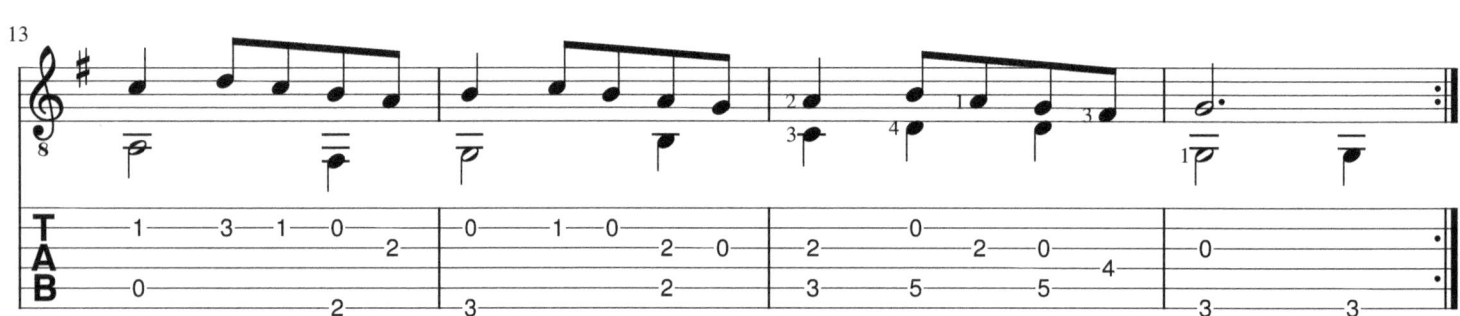

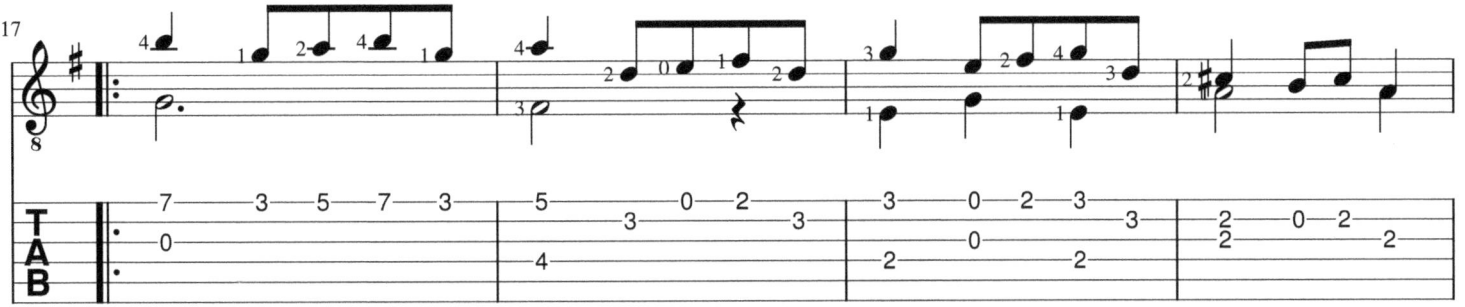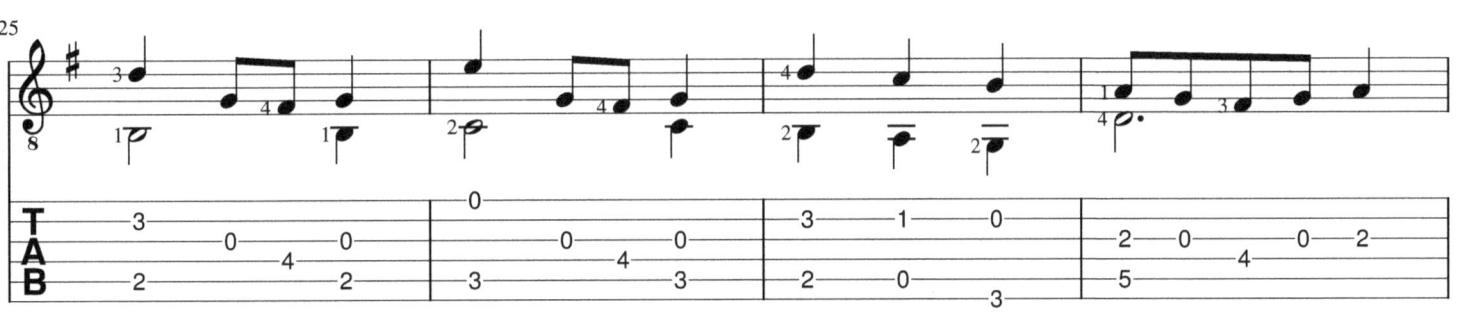

Bouree

Johann Sebastian Bach (1685-1750)

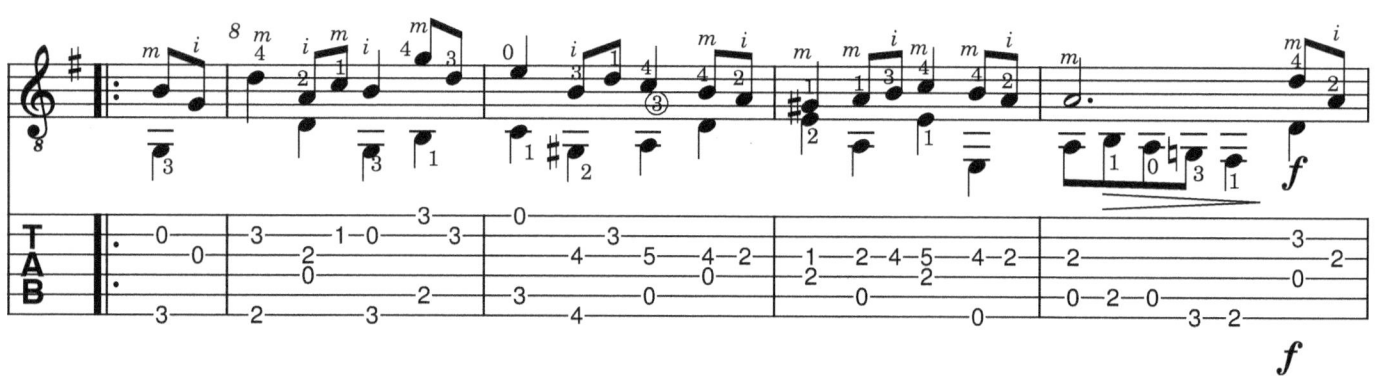
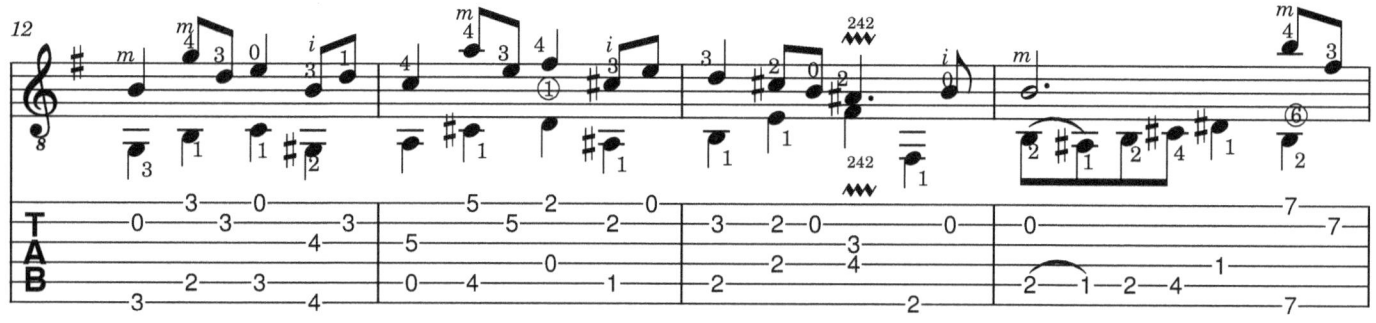

Gavotte (from suite 6 for cello, BWV 1012)

Johann Sebastian Bach (1685-1750)

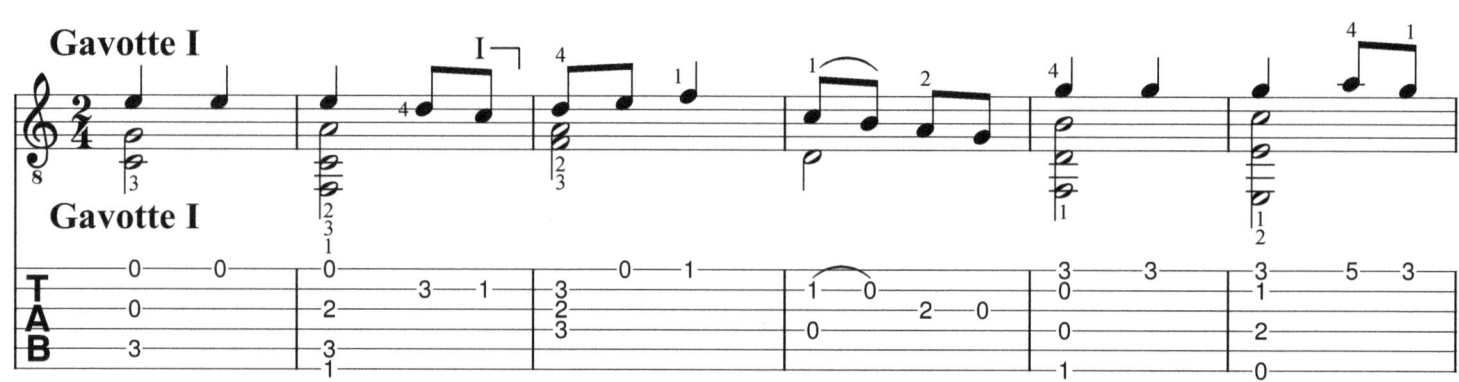
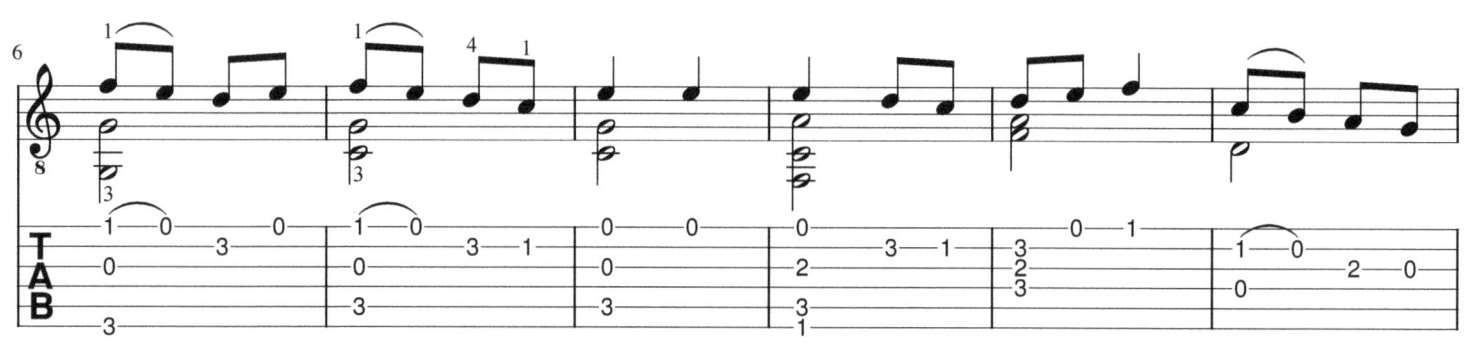
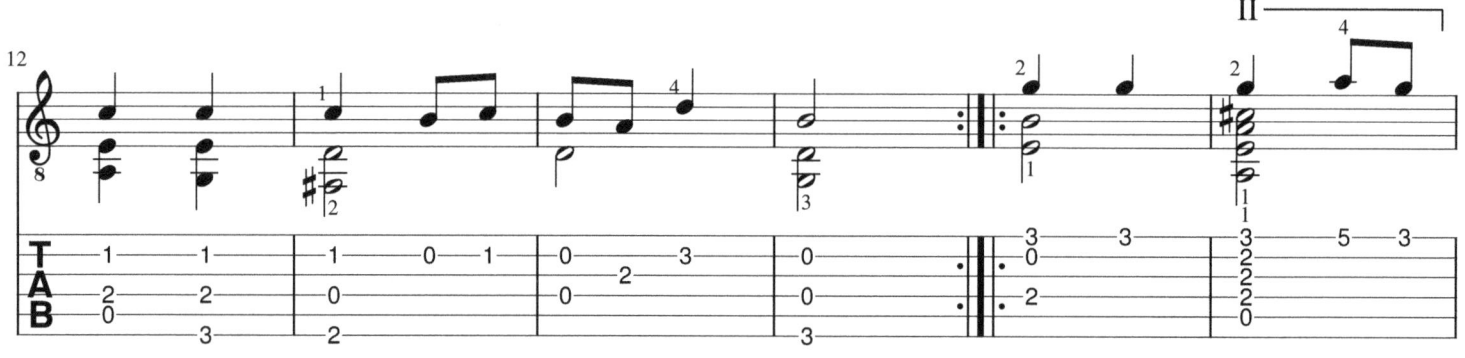

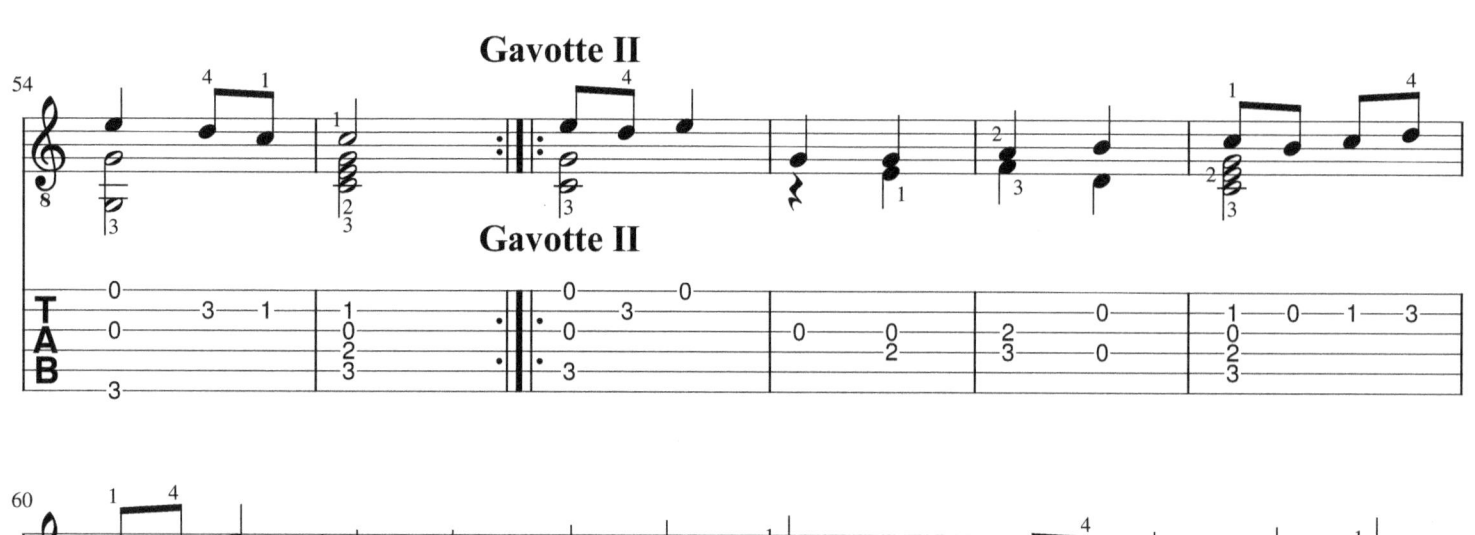

Gavotte II

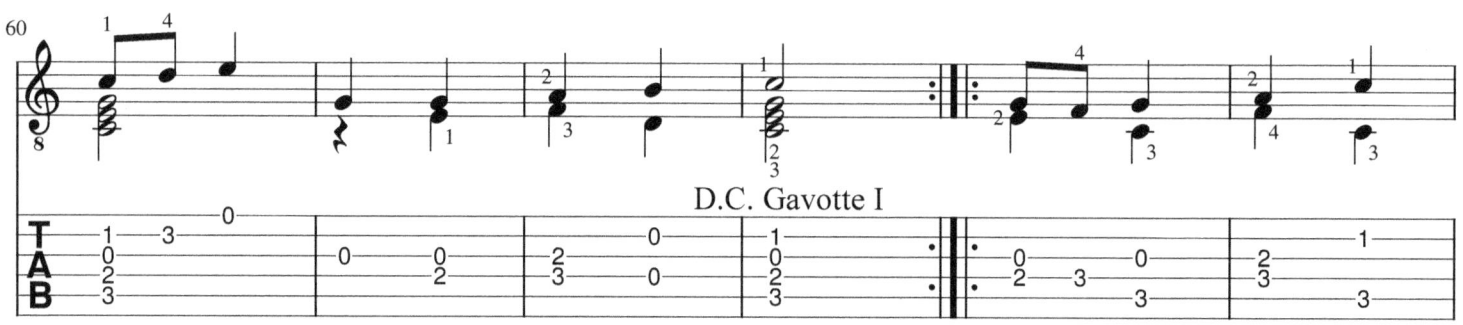

D.C. Gavotte I

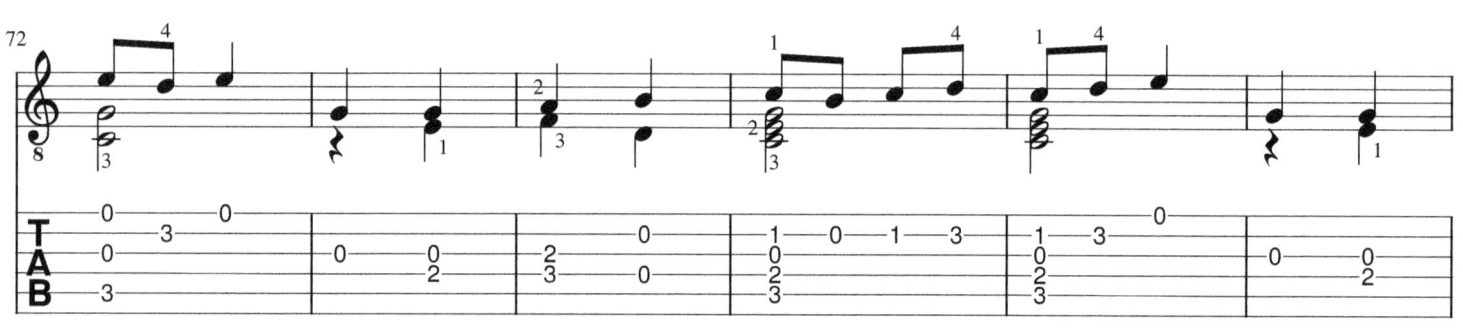

D.C. Gavotte I

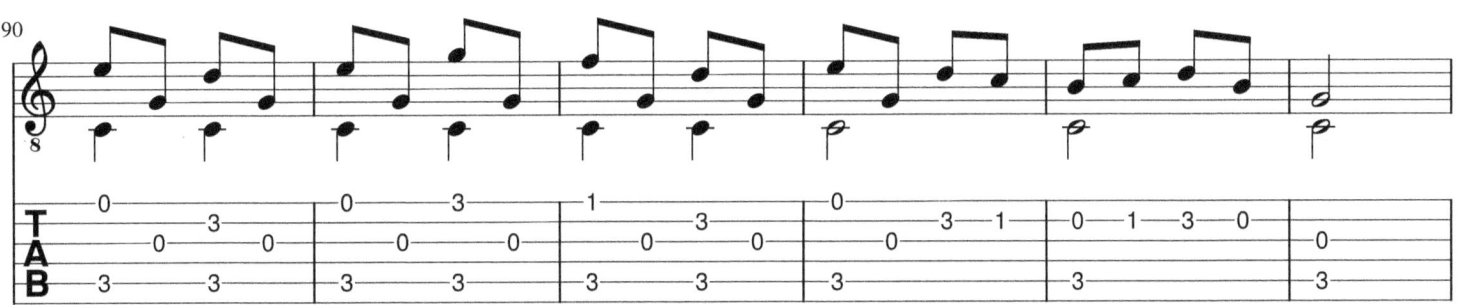
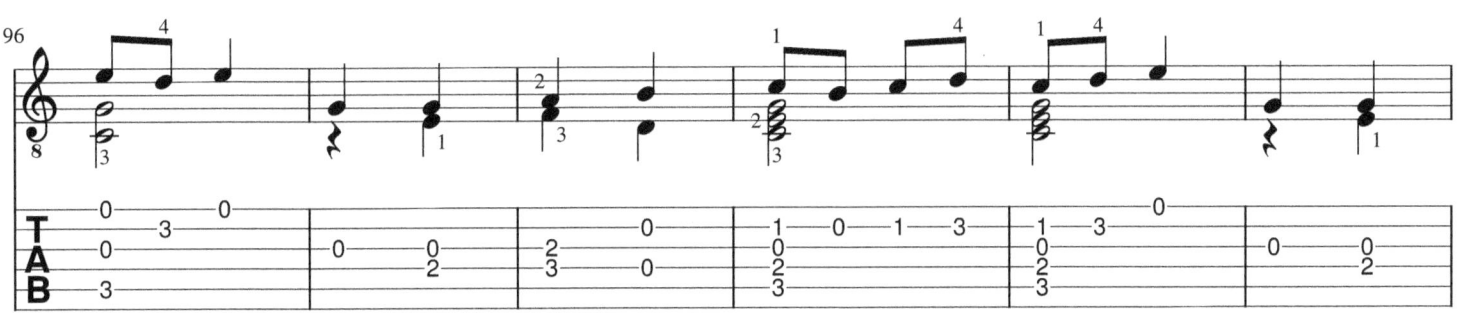
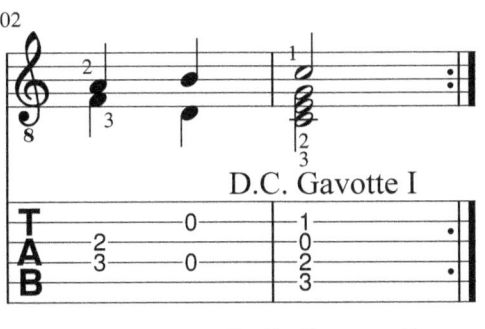

D.C. Gavotte I

Sarabande

Johann Sebastian Bach (1685-1750)

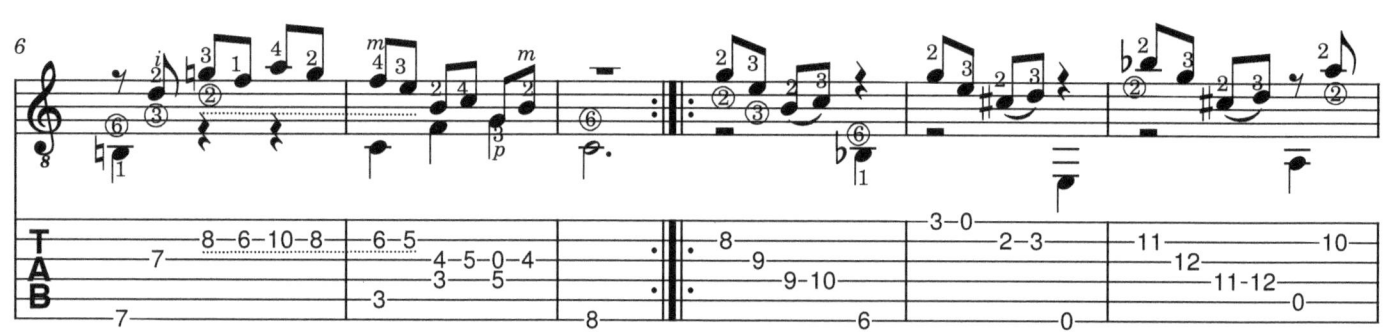
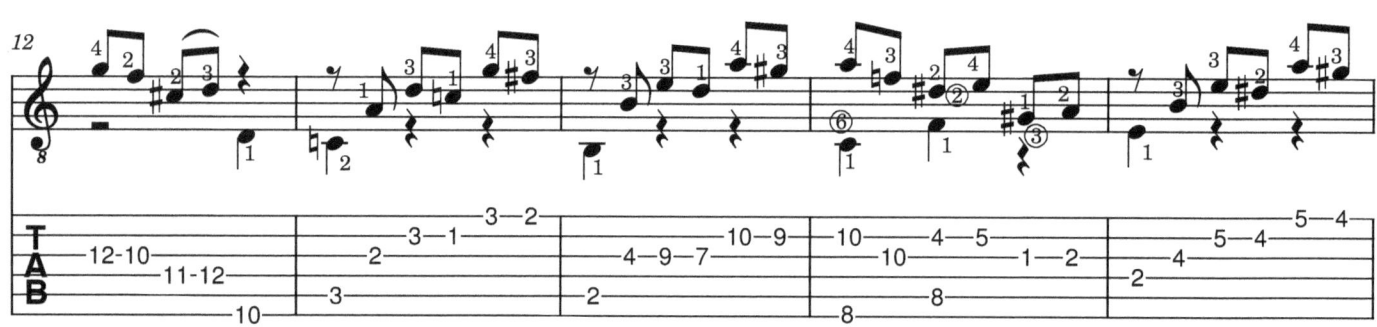
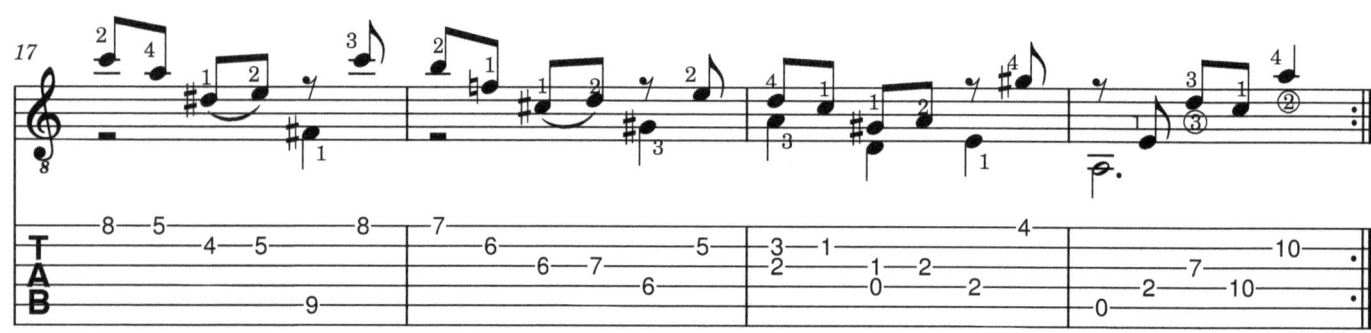

Preludium

Johann Sebastian Bach (1685-1750)

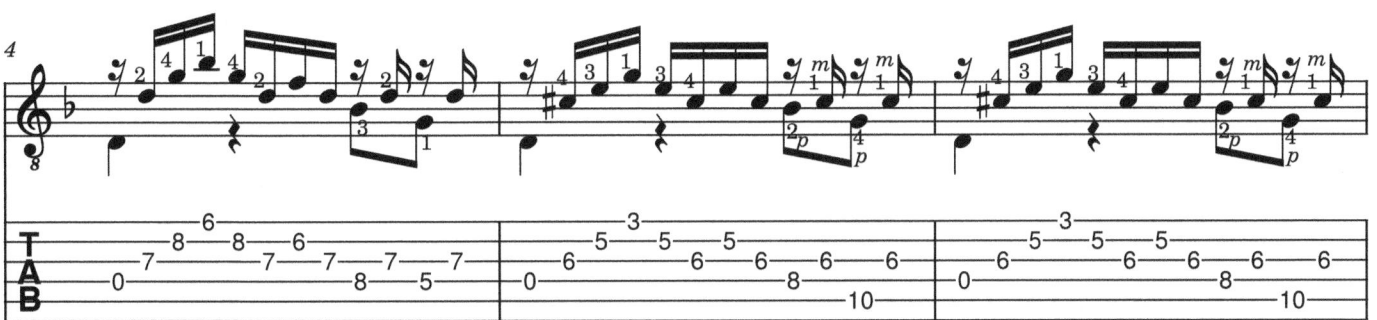
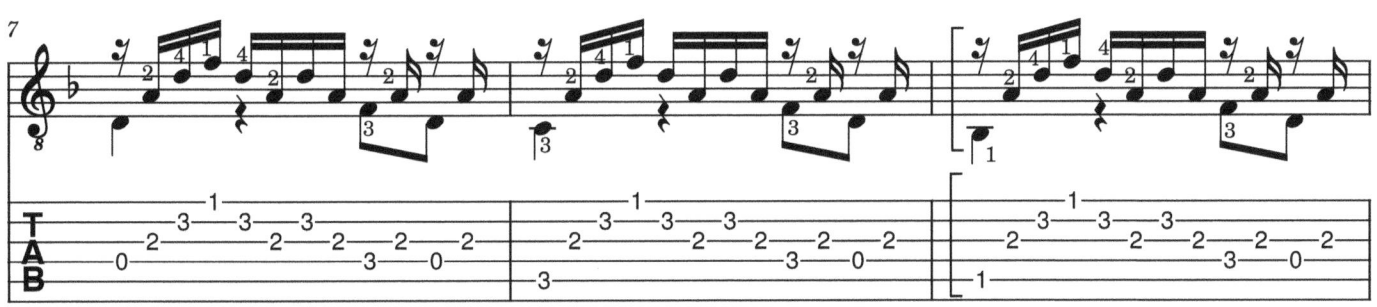

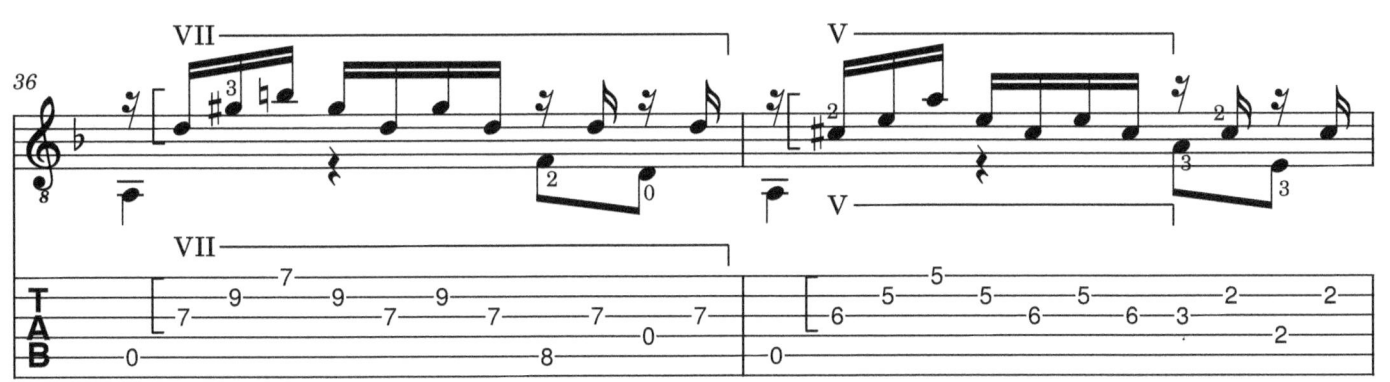

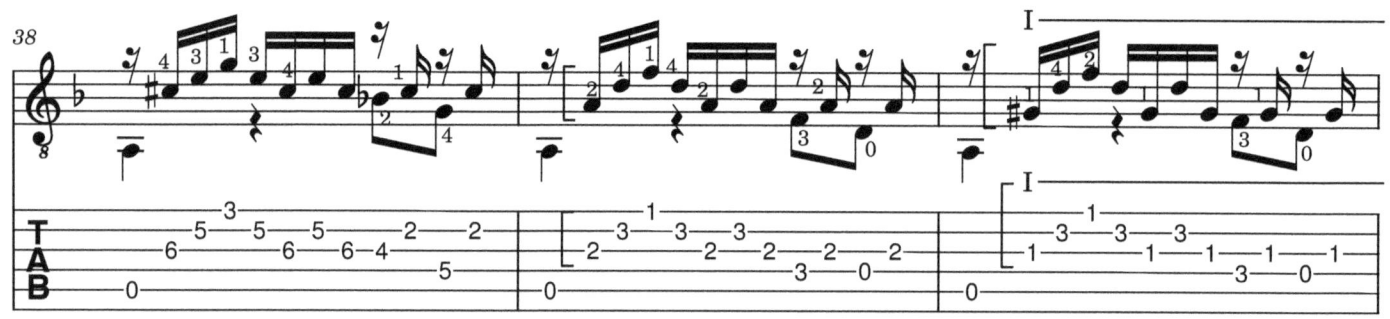
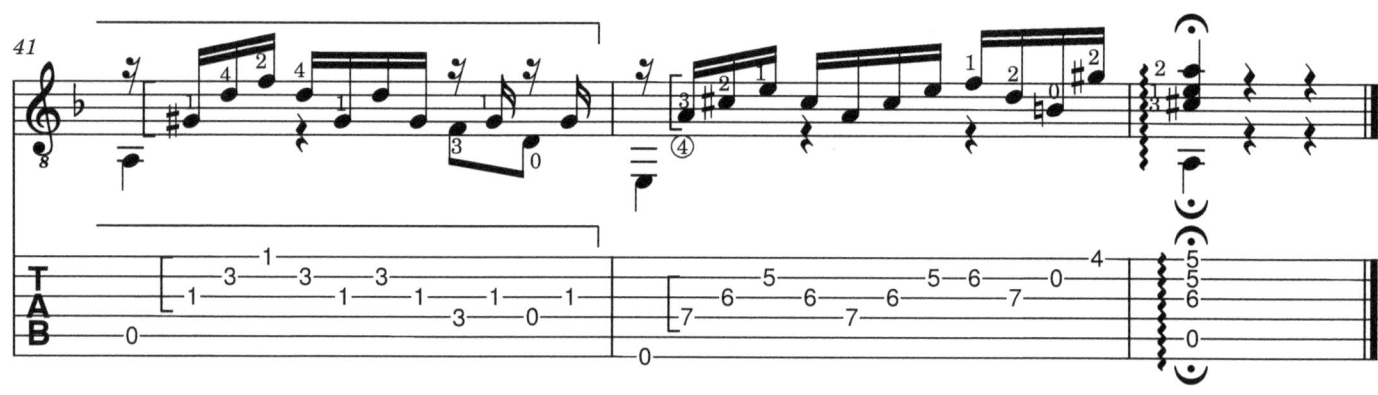

www.ingramcontent.com/pod-product-compliance
Lightning Source LLC
Chambersburg PA
CBHW041808070526
44585CB00026B/2883